The Scale Of... Animals

By Joanna Brundle

BookLife
PUBLISHING

©2019
BookLife Publishing Ltd.
King's Lynn
Norfolk PE30 4LS

All rights reserved.
Printed in Malaysia.

A catalogue record for this book is available from the British Library.

ISBN: 978-1-78637-883-5

Written by:
Joanna Brundle

Edited by:
Madeline Tyler

Designed by:
Jasmine Pointer

All facts, statistics, web addresses and URLs in this book were verified as valid and accurate at time of writing. No responsibility for any changes to external websites or references can be accepted by either the author or publisher.

Photocredits

All images courtesy of Shutterstock.com. With thanks to Getty Images, Thinkstock Photo and iStockphoto.

Front Cover – Keep Calm and Vector, Rvector, Colorlife, miniwide, Mountain Brothers, Marish, Nadya_Art, Aliaksei Hur, Tarikdiz, studio Martin, Deemak Daksina, T VECTOR ICONS, Sentavio, Bahruz Rzayev, miniwide. 4–5 – MarySan, Spreadthesign. 6–7 – Alevanda, sayu, Katflare, Usagi-P. 8–9 – AnnstasAg, matrioshka, Alfazet Chronicles. 10–11 – SaveJungle. 12–13 – Usagi-P, Nenilkime, Maquiladora. 14–15 – GraphicsRF, Vector Tradition. 16–17 – Zvereva Yana. 18–19 – Valeri Hadeev. 20–21 – BigMouse. 22–23 – Sunny_nsk, marinat197.

CONTENTS

Page 4	Introduction
Page 6	Cat Flea and Bee Hummingbird
Page 8	Bee Hummingbird, Ostrich and Capybara
Page 10	Capybara, Pygmy Jerboa and Giant Panda
Page 12	Giant Panda, Koala and Grey Wolf
Page 14	Grey Wolf and White Rhinoceros
Page 16	White Rhinoceros and Giraffe
Page 18	Giraffe and African Bush Elephant
Page 20	African Bush Elephant and Blue Whale
Page 22	Blue Whale and Krill
Page 24	Glossary and Index

Words that look like <u>this</u> can be found in the glossary on page 24.

INTRODUCTION

The scale of things means how one thing compares in size to another. In this book, we will be comparing many different kinds of animal by looking at their length, weight or height.

Height

Length

Animals come in all shapes and sizes, from tiny insects to huge <u>mammals</u>. Animals are found all over the world. Let's go on an animal hunt and start comparing.

We will be measuring the heights and lengths of different animals in metres. A door in your house or school is around two metres high. This should help you imagine how big and small these animals are.

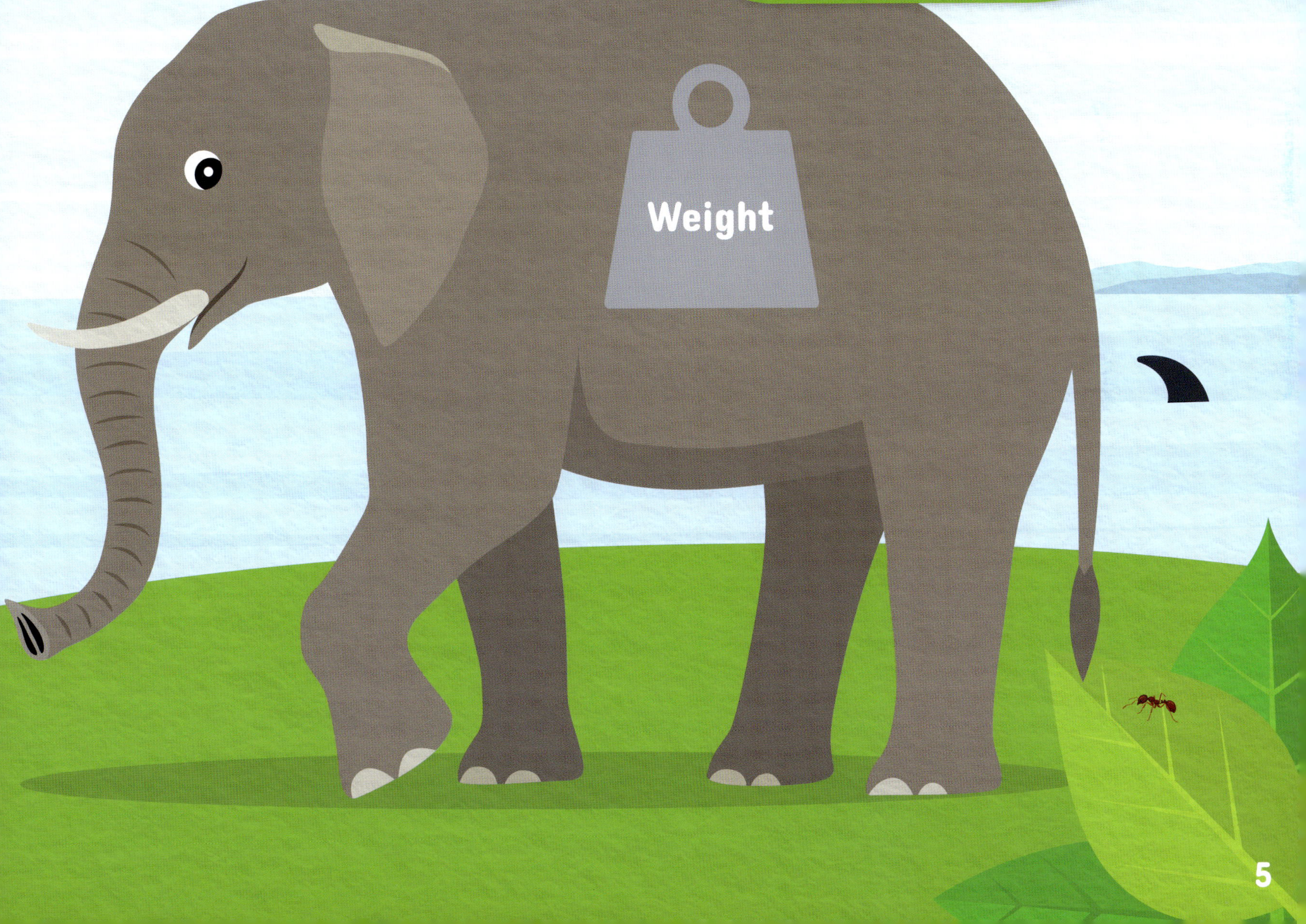

Weight

Cat Flea and Bee Hummingbird

Cat fleas are very small insects with no wings. They live on animals such as cats, dogs and badgers. Some cat fleas are less than one millimetre long, but others can be over three millimetres long. Females are larger than males.

One millimetre

Fleas are excellent jumpers and can jump many times their body length.

55 millimetres

The bee hummingbird is the world's smallest bird. The male is slightly smaller than the female. His body is around 55 millimetres in length, so he is about **17 TIMES LONGER** than a large cat flea.

Bee Hummingbird, Ostrich and Capybara

Bee hummingbirds can <u>hover</u> and fly forwards, backwards and even upside down. They flap their wings 80 times per second. Male bee hummingbirds usually weigh less than two grams.

The largest bird in the world, the ostrich, weighs around 145 kilograms. That's at least 72,500 TIMES more than the male bee hummingbird.

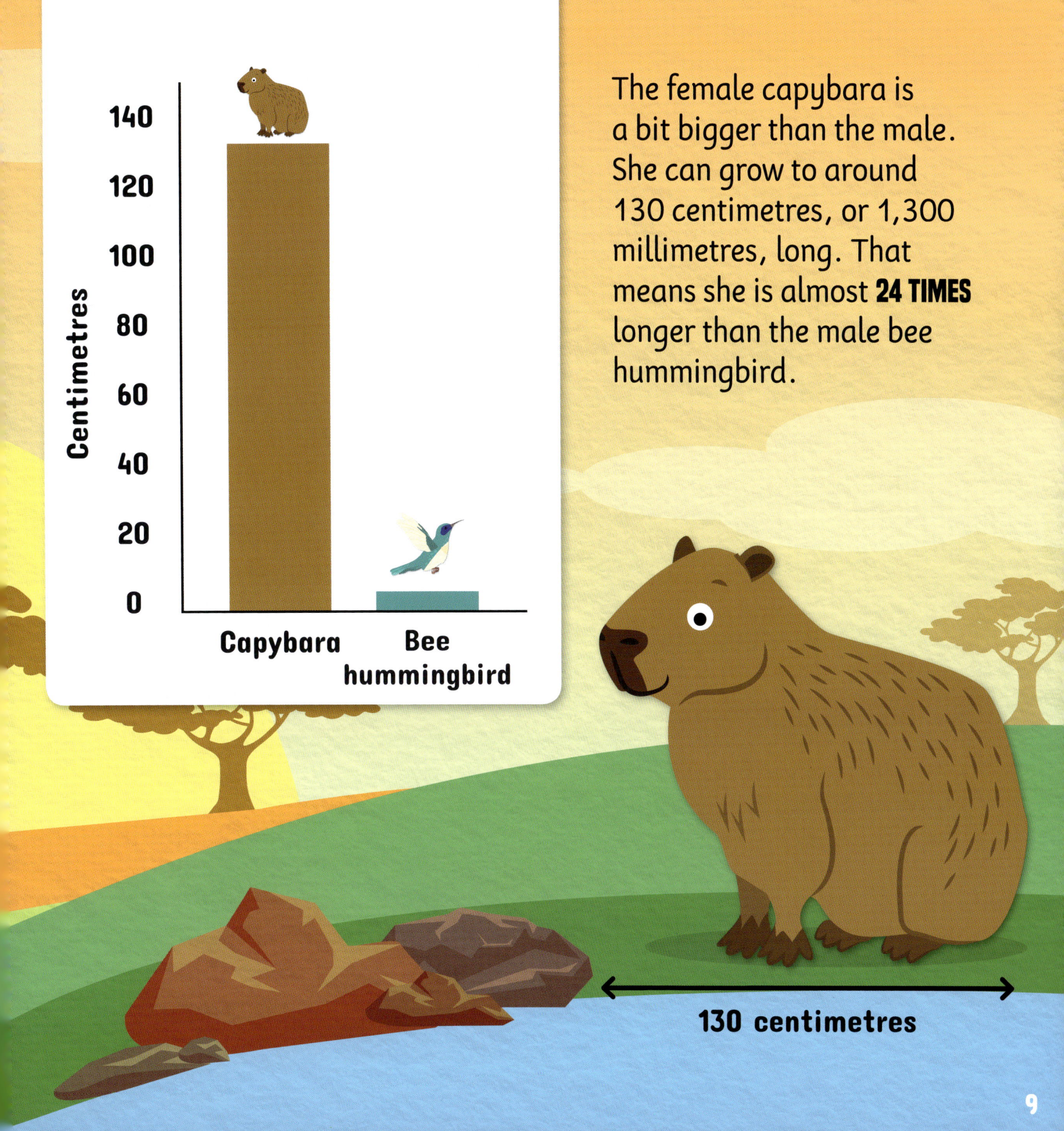

The female capybara is a bit bigger than the male. She can grow to around 130 centimetres, or 1,300 millimetres, long. That means she is almost **24 TIMES** longer than the male bee hummingbird.

CAPYBARA, PYGMY JERBOA AND GIANT PANDA

The capybara is the largest <u>rodent</u> in the world. It can weigh up to 65 kilograms. It has partly <u>webbed feet</u> that help it to swim and paddle in rivers and marshes.

The pygmy jerboa weighs only three grams and is the smallest rodent in the world.

22 centimetres 130 centimetres

150 centimetres

The male giant panda can grow to a length of around 150 centimetres. That's almost the same length as one female capybara and four male bee hummingbirds.

Giant Panda, Koala and Grey Wolf

The giant panda lives in bamboo forests in the mountains of China. It has a thick, woolly coat to keep it warm. Pandas are good at climbing trees and can also swim.

A male giant panda can weigh up to 150 kilograms. That is more than 11 TIMES the weight of an adult male koala.

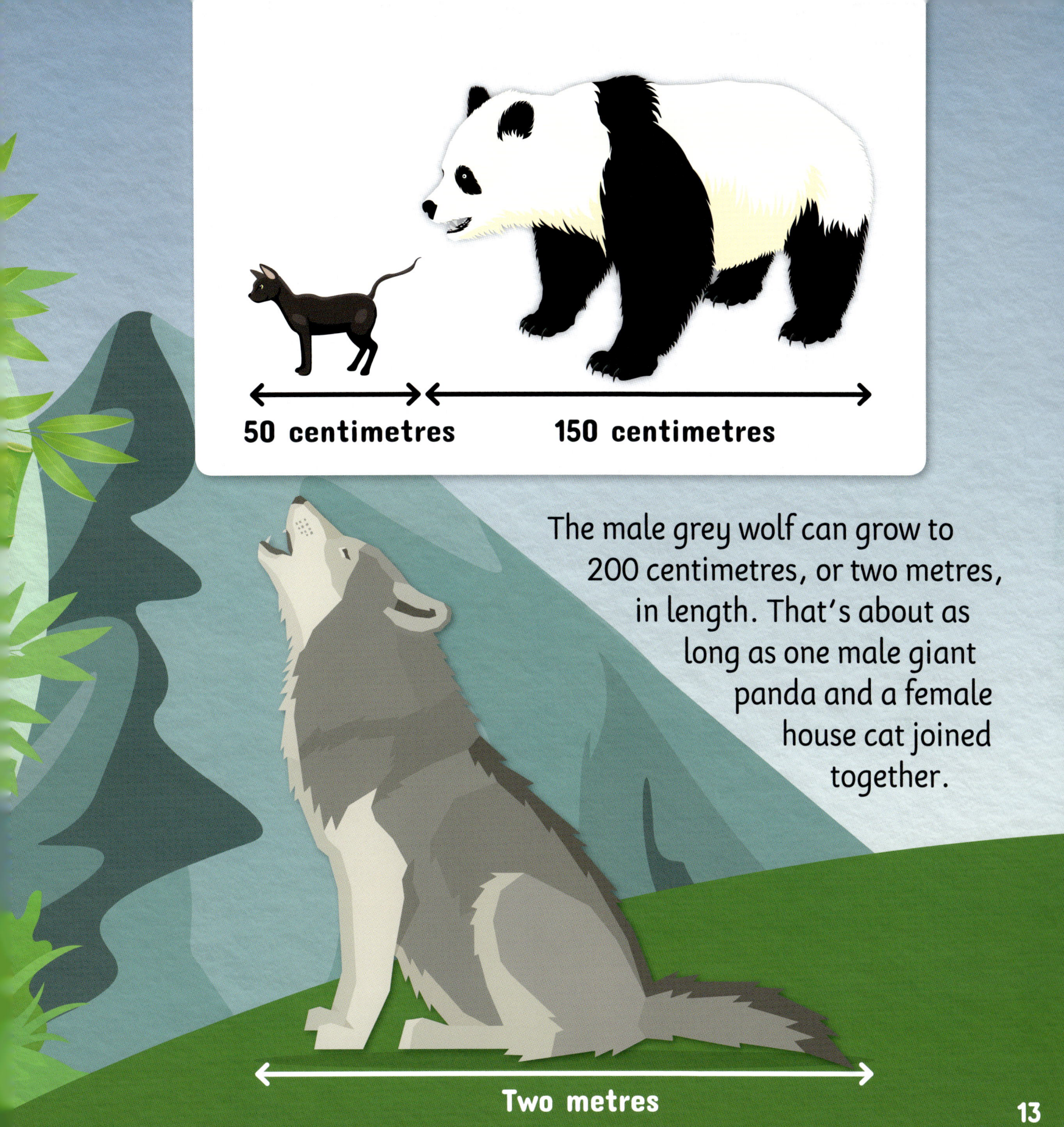

50 centimetres   **150 centimetres**

The male grey wolf can grow to 200 centimetres, or two metres, in length. That's about as long as one male giant panda and a female house cat joined together.

Two metres

Grey Wolf and White Rhinoceros

An adult male grey wolf can weigh up to 79 kilograms. The male giant panda is nearly twice as heavy as a grey wolf.

Grey wolves live and hunt in groups called packs. Wolves howl to communicate, or 'talk', with one another and with other packs.

The male white rhinoceros can grow to 400 centimetres, or four metres, in length. It is twice as long as a male grey wolf.

Metres

WHITE RHINOCEROS AND GIRAFFE

The male white rhinoceros weighs around 2,300 kilograms. That's heavier than 15 giant pandas.

The white rhinoceros has two horns on the top of its nose. The name 'rhinoceros' means 'nose horn'. Rhinos love to wallow in muddy pools to keep cool.

The male giraffe can grow to a height of five and a half metres. Its height is equal to the length of one male white rhinoceros and one male giant panda joined together.

GIRAFFE
AND
AFRICAN BUSH ELEPHANT

The giraffe is the tallest land animal. It has a very long neck, hairy lips and large eyes. Each animal's skin <u>markings</u> are different. Giraffes can gallop at speeds of up to 50 kilometres per hour.

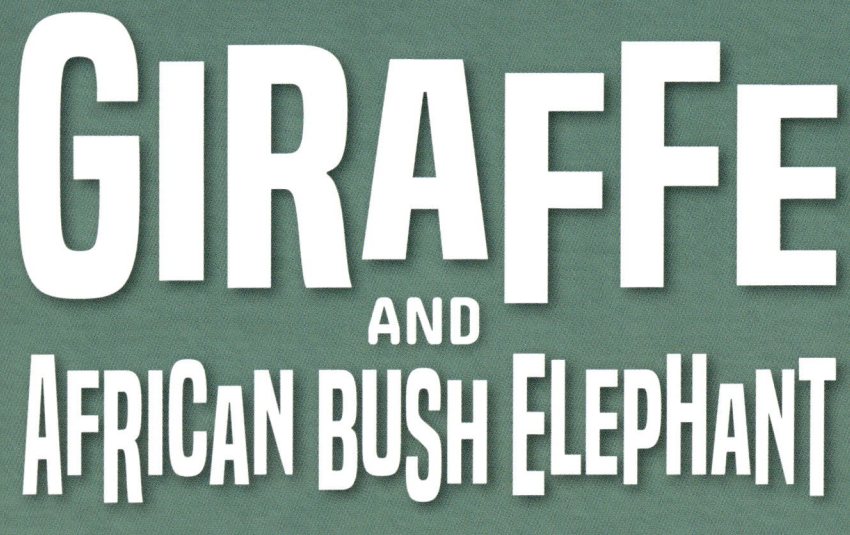

A giraffe is taller than three adult humans standing on one another's heads.

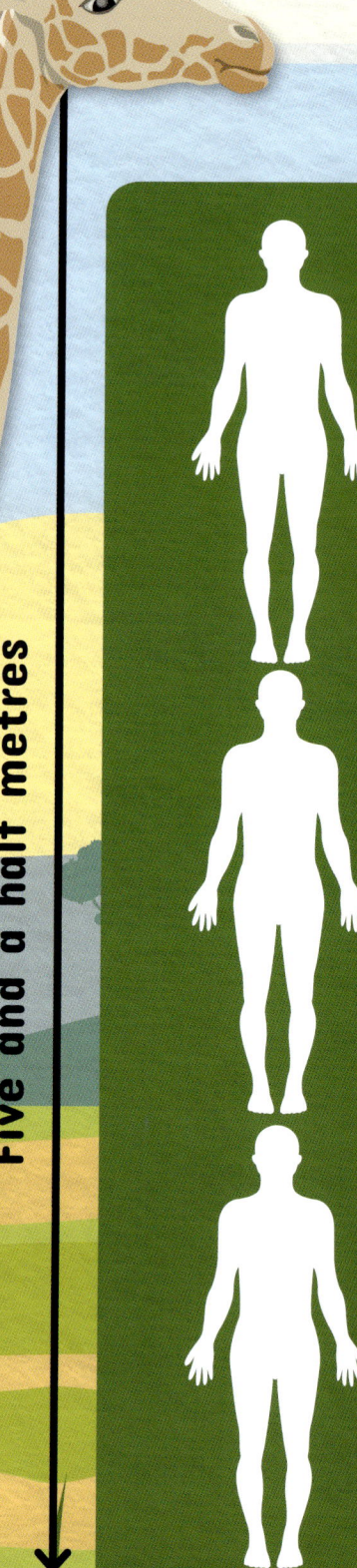

Five and a half metres

The African bush elephant is the largest land animal. The male can grow to over seven metres long. That's longer than the height of one giraffe and the length of one male giant panda joined together.

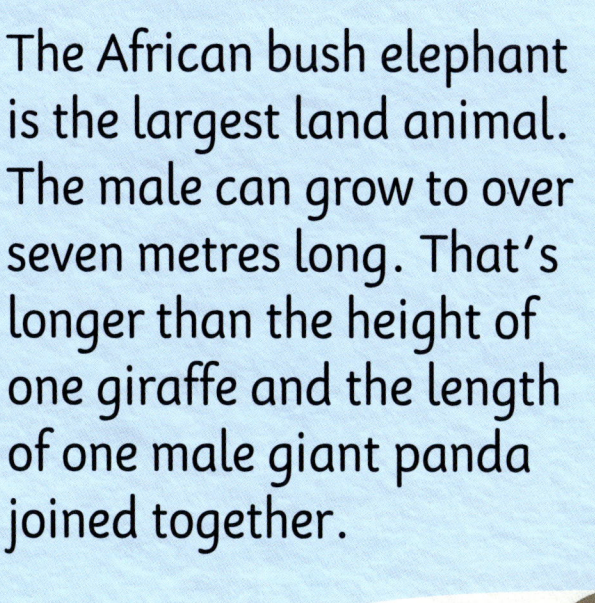

150 centimetres

Five and a half metres

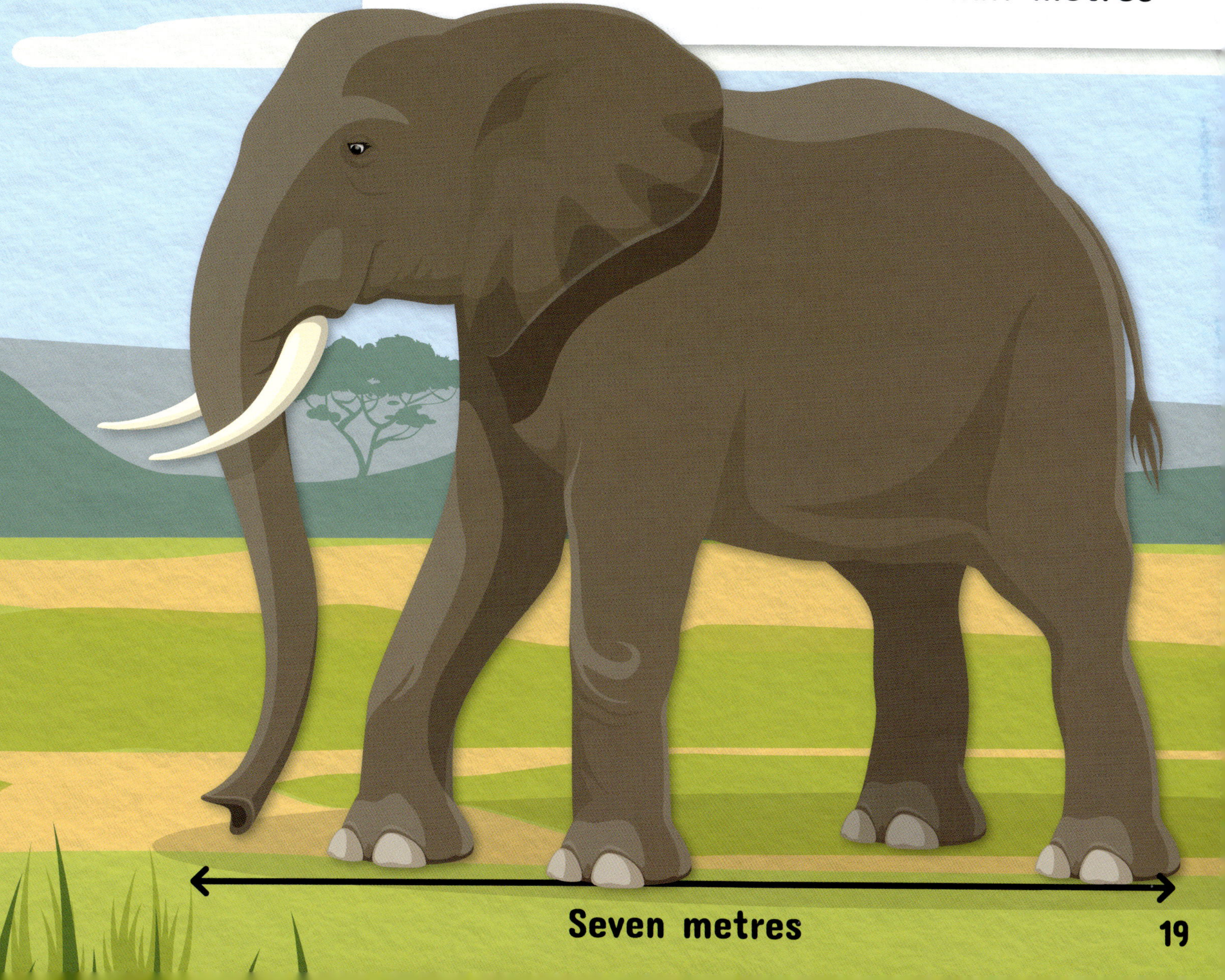

Seven metres

African Bush Elephant and Blue Whale

African bush elephants spend most of their day eating plants and fruit. They use their trunks to throw sand and mud over themselves to protect their skin from the hot sun.

The male African bush elephant can weigh up to 6,350 kilograms. That is nearly three times as much as the male white rhinoceros.

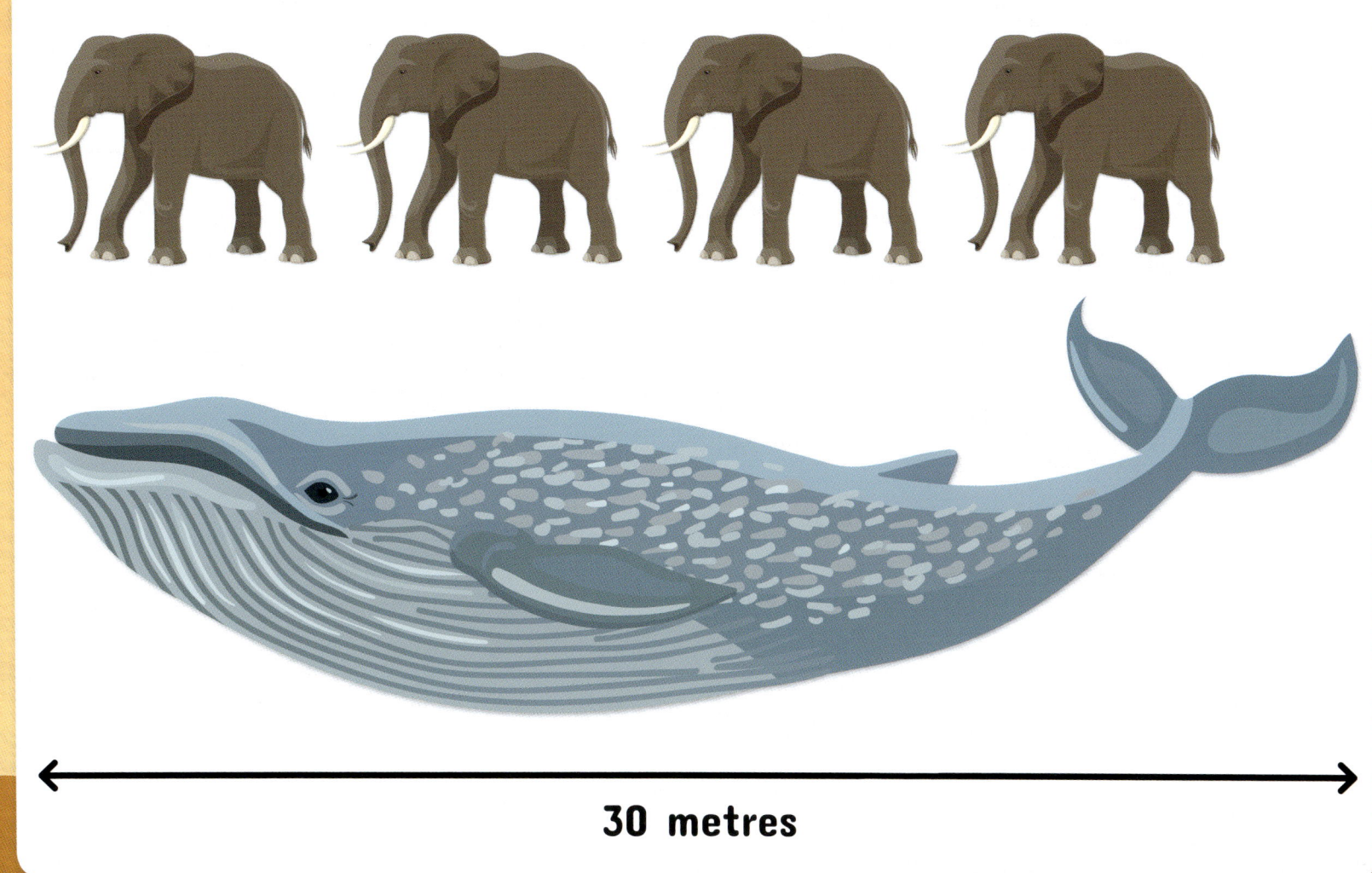

30 metres

The blue whale can grow to a length of over 30 metres. That's longer than four male African bush elephants joined together. Female blue whales are usually bigger than the males.

Blue Whale
and Krill

The blue whale is the largest animal in the world. Despite its size, it eats tiny, shrimp-like creatures called krill. Krill are just 50–60 millimetres long, about the same size as the bee hummingbird we saw on pages 7, 8 and 9.

The female blue whale can weigh over 181,000 kilograms. That's the weight of around 134 small cars.

In one day, a blue whale can eat 3,600 kilograms of krill. That's the same weight as 24 giant pandas.

GLOSSARY

bamboo	a giant, woody grass that is the main food of the giant panda
horns	hard, pointed growths found on the head of some animals
hover	to stay in the air in one place
howl	to make a long, loud wailing sound
mammals	animals that have warm blood and a backbone and produce milk
markings	marks or patterns of marks on an animal's fur or skin
rodent	a mammal with sharp front teeth used for gnawing
wallow	to roll about or lie in water or mud
webbed feet	feet in which the toes are joined together by a thin fold of skin

INDEX

African bush elephants 19–21
bee hummingbirds 7–9, 11, 22
blue whales 21–23
capybaras 9–11

cat fleas 6–7
giant pandas 11–14, 16–17, 19, 23
giraffes 17–19
grey wolves 13–15
humans 18

koalas 12
krill 22–23
ostriches 8
pygmy jerboas 10
white rhinoceroses 15–17, 20